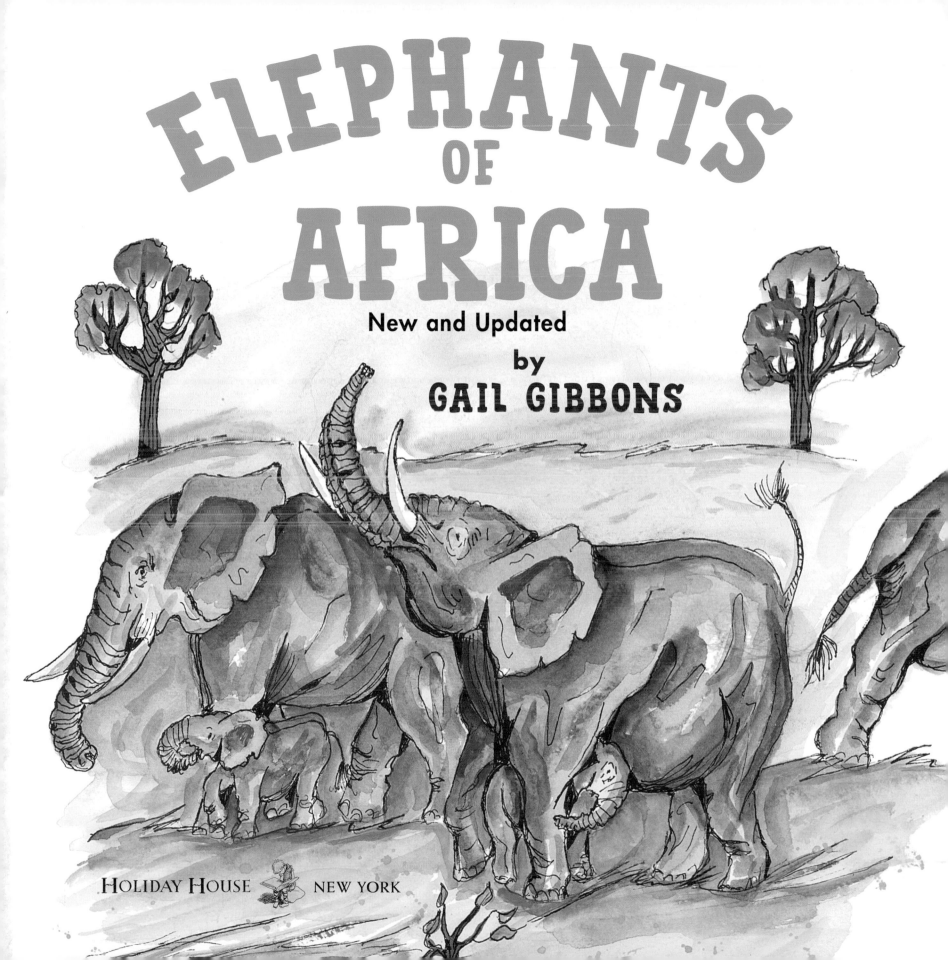

ELEPHANTS
OF
AFRICA

New and Updated

by
GAIL GIBBONS

HOLIDAY HOUSE • NEW YORK

To Lorenzo Buttignol

Special thanks to Jim Doherty, General Curator Emeritus of the New York Zoological Society, Bronx, New York.

Thanks also to Sara Ketelson of the Mammology Department,
American Museum of Natural History.

A SAVANNA is a large grassland with scattered trees.

A HERD is a group of the same kind of animals.

A herd of African elephants makes its way across the vast savanna. Elephants are the largest living land animals.

3

African elephants also live in forests.

AREAS IN AFRICA WHERE MOST ELEPHANTS LIVE

AFRICA

ATLANTIC OCEAN

INDIAN OCEAN

The mammoth and the mastodon were prehistoric members of the elephant family that lived in the last Ice Age. They both had thick fur to protect them from the cold.

AFRICAN ELEPHANT CHARACTERISTICS

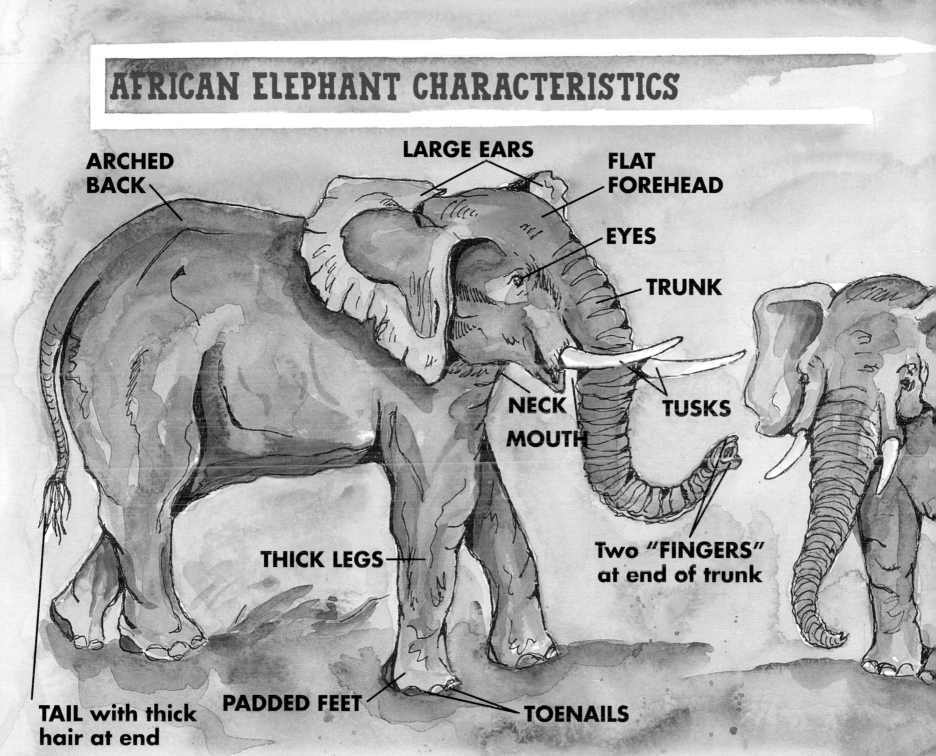

ARCHED BACK

LARGE EARS

FLAT FOREHEAD

EYES

TRUNK

NECK

MOUTH

TUSKS

Two "FINGERS" at end of trunk

THICK LEGS

PADDED FEET

TOENAILS

TAIL with thick hair at end

A male African elephant can grow to be 13 feet (3.9 meters) tall and weigh as much as 7 tons (6.3 metric tons). Females are smaller and grow up to be 8.7 feet tall (2.6 meters) and weigh about 4 tons (3.6 metric tons).

AN ELEPHANT'S TRUNK

The trunk has around 40,000 muscles. The "fingers" at the end of the trunk are so sensitive that they can pick a leaf off a tree.

SMELLING

DRINKING

The trunk of an elephant is a combination of its nose and its upper lip. It is strong and flexible and has many uses.

8

COMMUNICATING

EATING

REACHING AND PULLING

DIGGING

SHOWERING

SNORKELING

AN ELEPHANT'S TUSKS

TUSKS

STRIPPING OFF BARK FOR FOOD

DIGGING FOR WATER

DIGGING UP ROOTS FOR FOOD

Tusks are large teeth that grow out of each side of the upper jaw. An elephant uses its tusks in many different ways.

MALES BATTLING OVER A POSSIBLE MATE

Tusks start to grow when an elephant is very young and continue to grow throughout its life. They can be as long as 11 feet (3.3 meters) and weigh more than 200 pounds (90.7 kilograms).

AN ELEPHANT'S SKIN

THICK SKIN

Most of the skin of an elephant is about 1.5 inches (3.8 centimeters) thick to protect the elephant from its harsh environment. When it is very hot, elephants roll and wallow in mud and blow sand or soil over their backs to form mud packs. This protects their skin from sunburn and helps keep their bodies cooler.

The end of a TAIL has coarse hairs up to 30 inches (76.2 centimeters) long.

To help protect their sensitive skin from flies and other biting insects, elephants will shower themselves with water, sand, or soil. They may also use their tails to swat away these pests.

AN ELEPHANT'S EARS

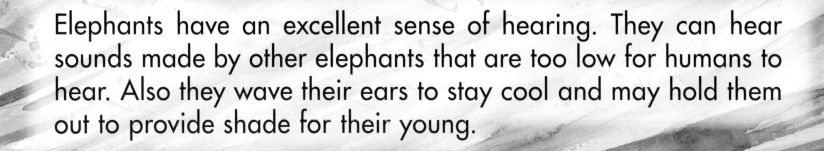

Elephants have an excellent sense of hearing. They can hear sounds made by other elephants that are too low for humans to hear. Also they wave their ears to stay cool and may hold them out to provide shade for their young.

AN ELEPHANT'S EYES

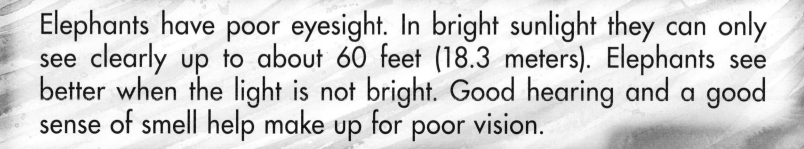

Elephants have poor eyesight. In bright sunlight they can only see clearly up to about 60 feet (18.3 meters). Elephants see better when the light is not bright. Good hearing and a good sense of smell help make up for poor vision.

AN ELEPHANT'S TEETH

An elephant may grow up to six sets of molars during their lifetime. The last set of molars come in when the elephant is around 30–40 years old.

A MOLAR is usually about 10 inches (25.4 centimeters) by 2 inches (5.1 centimeters) by 2 inches (5.1 centimeters).

An elephant eats by using its four molar teeth to grind food. Elephants in the wild may eat more than 300 pounds (136 kilograms) of food in a day. They eat branches, grasses, leaves, bark, roots, fruits, and berries.

An adult male is called a BULL.

With gentle reassurance, a mother helps her calf stand up on its feet.

An adult female is called a COW.

A baby elephant is called a CALF.

A CALF usually weighs 200 pounds (90.7 kilograms) and stands about 3 feet (.9 meter) tall at birth.

When it is mating time, males may compete for the attention of a female. The females usually mate every four to five years. About 22 months after mating, the female gives birth.

For about two years the young calf will need to drink gallons of its mother's milk every day. At two years old, it will continue to nurse plus begin to eat leaves and other grown-up foods that its mother is eating. At about four or five years old, it will be completely weaned off its mother's milk.

On rare occasions, family groups may include adopted orphans.

Elephants are social animals and live in family groups of about six to twelve elephants. The adults are all females, usually a mother and her daughters. The rest are their calves of varying ages. The members of the group stay together.

Young male elephants joust and play with one another, learning how to defend themselves when they go out on their own. They usually leave the family group at about twelve to fifteen years of age and live with other young bull elephants.

By the age of twenty-five to thirty-five years old, a bull elephant is likely to be living on its own, but usually not far from family groups.

Females stay with their family group and help to raise the young. When the group gets too big, one or two adult females, usually sisters, go off with their calves. Together they start a new family group.

The family group is led by a matriarch, usually the eldest and most experienced female. She knows her home range, how to find food and water, and how to avoid enemies.

FINDING FOOD

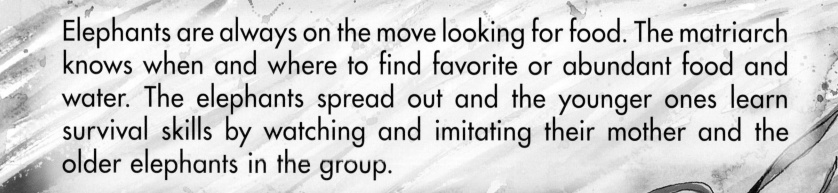

Elephants are always on the move looking for food. The matriarch knows when and where to find favorite or abundant food and water. The elephants spread out and the younger ones learn survival skills by watching and imitating their mother and the older elephants in the group.

Elephants have been known to carry food
to old or sickly elephants that are unable to
forage on their own.

Elephants spend most of the
day and night feeding or
looking for their next meal.

Elephants don't like to be separated from one another. When they come back together, they greet one another by flapping their ears, making screeching and trumpeting sounds, and winding their trunks together with affection.

When the food in an area is gone, family groups may join together and form a herd. They move on.

FINDING WATER

An elephant sucks up about 2.5 gallons (9.46 liters) of water into its trunk and then blows the water into its mouth. It may drink about 50 gallons (200 liters) a day.

Young ones squeal as they fill their trunks and squirt one another.

They wallow in the mud to stay cool. This protects them from the sun and annoying insects.

Elephants need a lot of water.

When water is not readily available, the matriarch is said to be able to smell water under the ground miles away. She will use her tusks and front feet to dig down into the earth, starting a watering hole. This will benefit other animals as well.

The elephants make loud trumpeting sounds.

They spread their ears to make themselves look bigger.

They gather around the young ones to protect them.

Other than humans, elephants' only enemies are hyenas and lions, which have been known to kill baby elephants. The scent of a lion or hyena strikes fear in all elephants. If they can't get away, the whole group will do what is necessary to keep the calves safe.

POACHERS are people who hunt illegally. They normally poach elephants just to take the ivory tusks. Don't buy elephant ivory!

PRESERVE

Elephants are threatened by expanding human settlements and by poachers. Nature preserves have been created. Wardens are there to help protect the elephants from poachers. These special animals deserve respect and consideration.

ELEPHANT TRACKS

Elephants are found in warm climates. They don't have a layer of fat to protect them from freezing temperatures.

Elephants can walk very quietly because they have thick pads on the bottoms of their feet.

An elephant can move as fast as 18 to 25 miles per hour (28.9–40.2 kilometers).

In the wild, elephants may live to be more than sixty years old.

Elephants usually sleep standing up for about three to four hours a day.

Elephants can swim for hours and go several miles.

Ninety-nine percent of baby elephants are born at night.